EVERYDAY MERMAID

EVERYDAY MERMAID

POEMS BY CHRISTINA ISOBEL

ART BY DEIDRE SCHERER

a thousand flowers ™
PO BOX 460339, San Francisco, CA 94114-9992
info@athousandflowers.org
www.athousandflowers.org

Printed by GSL in Sacramento, California
Library of Congress Control Number 2018907839
ISBN 978-1-949824-00-1

Deidre and I dedicate this book to the environment with the deepest conviction that discovering and honoring our personal connection to nature changes how we treat the earth and brings us back to ourselves. To harm the earth is to break the thread of our lives.

For Robert Bly, Mirabai, and Emily Dickinson, who showed me fairytales, rubies, evanescent wings, and a way of life. And to my daughters, Arwen and Meara, who taught me love.
—CHRISTINA ISOBEL

For my grandchildren, Tyler, Scott, Matt, Shayla, Michelle, Aaron, Kai, Elyas, Lidianna, Lucas, and Ariella, who teach me the flow of life.
—DEIDRE SCHERER

CONTENTS

PROLOGUE

This book began in a simple way. The poems began coming, and as I wrote them, I realized they were about valuing everyday life, the life that happens at home and around the house from moment to moment, day to night, season to season, around the year. As I wrote and listened, a discovery happened. I learned that those moments could spark, in an instant, a form of grace that connected me to myself, and to something bigger than myself—to the world—and that grace can happen at any instant.

A play I've been working on about St. Francis and Emily Dickinson, both nature mystics, showed me that they knew this grace. Fascinated by most of creation, they embraced almost everything, from the sun, moon, and stars, to storms and rogue waves, to brambles, flowers, and trees, to wolves, bears, snakes, and flies, to their own bodies, their own diseases, and their own death. They swam in the mystic sea, whose waters bathed and nourished them.

I do not live there. Painful experiences swamp me, as they do most people. But through my poems, I learned that openness to all of life helps us float on that sea a bit more, gives us a bit more levity. And it gives us glimpses of the overwhelming love and joy, which is always ours.

Mermaids swim in that sea...

A FAIRYTAIL

Older I am
As I sit in the bathtub
To sleep
I'm done—no rest
For now.

I start to stand
Pull myself up
By the spigot,
But remember my wounded hip.
I turn around
Get on my hands and knees
Legs together
Push—through—water.
Up I emerge a Mermaid
On my fins
From a journey
In the dark sea.

A MERMAID'S JOURNEY INTO SLEEP

Hand folded upon hand
Knees tucked
Eyes closed—I wait for sleep to press me
Change my shape
My inner line releases
Travels up, then down
Abdominal core sinks in
Diaphragm so thin, so tight
Bursts to petals.

The dark behind my eyes succumbs
To a whirligig of...

Violet vectors
Shooting greens
Pulsing blues
Bending into
Brocades, beads
Necklaces, jewels.

A dress emerges, floating white
Light as air, no sleeves
Coming towards me
Fabric falls to my feet
In folds so gentle
Silver gems around my middle.

I walk softly
The dress sways with me
I enter a tunnel and see
Light before me.

I surrender.

GETTING TO SNOW

I keep a package in my brain
In the middle on the right
Full of poems written
In the night.

3 AM
Standing in the shower
A wall of water slides down my back.
As I look out the window
This January night
A blanket of moonlight
Is cast upon the meadow.
Again, again, again

Shimmering particles
Fall from the sky.
Oh, the magic in this world.

I go to bed and dream of snow.

DAY IN FOUR PARTS

I began the day in a car accident
Hit my left rear fender.

It wasn't a bad accident
   A little scrape
   A little rattled
   A bit shaken.

Home I ask my husband
For a hug
And cling to him like a
Starfish stuck to a rock
   On the brink of the sea.

Lying in bed
At the end of the day
I am a fish
In muddy water.

MORNING

Early morning shower
I hold up my hand
More in shadows than light.
I spread my fingers.
Feel the skin stretching—
Webbed like a duck.
More darkness inside.
Without, the white light
Slowly spreads
On the curve of the earth.

I FELT HIM ON MY BODY

Did I tell you a blue jay
Has been following me
For weeks?
Soft cow-brown head
Kingfisher crown
Iridescent blues in deep
Cloak him.

He first discovered me
In the breakfast nook
In the kitchen
Yellow trim
Around the windows.

He looked in
As I sat
Eating my cereal
Of seeds and oats.

Cracks, explosions
In my middle
Fluttering peacock eyes
Trembles on my lips
After a start and a try
A balk and a stammer
I skidded to a halt.
One day
I would
Die.

He followed me
To the window seat
Sat out on the rim
Of the wooden rail
Looked at me
With cold eyes
Looked away
I did too.

As he turned his head
Towards me
And I did him
I could feel
The glide
Of bone to bone
Upon his neck
Feathers
Ruffling on my skin
His wings
When they pushed up
Caught the wind
And the gap
He left
Behind.

A WOMAN'S JOY

A hummingbird
Whirs up out of
The nasturtium
Leaves
Turns around the
Bend
Dives straight In—
To that ripe repast
Of orange bell.
How sweet it is
To be a flower.

GARDEN

There is a large, single-petaled, yellow Mermaid Rose
    In our garden.
We decided to fill it up with vegetables:
Peas carrots cabbages asparagus lettuces kale collards
    corn purslane squashes tomatoes—I could go on...
I decided to have a design.
    I'd do it myself.
    It must have a focal point
I thought thinking of a water feature: a pond, a fountain, or perhaps
    A dial for the sun, or an alcove with curvaceous paths.
But then I thought, looked; looked, thought, realized:
The garden is not that large.
Perhaps a bench here, a bench there, a path near the side.
My husband sighed.
    There's not that much room, he said.
    I remembered:
There is a mermaid in our garden.
She can grow up to six feet wide.

AN IRIS

Tight small bud of black
An iris to be
I wait a day, then another
For the Shivery Mystery.

I come back
A curl, a lip, a scalloped edge
Not dark, but lavender.

Disappointed I do not stay,
But go away and then...
Walking by so casually—

Unfurling fronds of rainbows shoot
Purples, gold, and rose
In iridescent splendor.

THE RIDER

I've seen bicycle riders all day
Two wheels on the road
In perfect tandem
Straight line
Rider melds with bike with ground
And swings across the lanes
To the other side.

Later
I stood outside
In the middle
Of my
Asphalt driveway
And looked up.
A wind commenced
To blow.
And the trees...

The time was dusk
The magic time
Of special light
And prepubescent air.
Of shadows and setting bright
Chills and warmth.

The trees
Became
Not a breath apart
Not a hair
One unit
One sound
One beat.
They moved
Like a rider
A massive dark rider
In the sky.
To and fro
Side to side.

With eyes closed
I began to feel
A hum in me
Tuning me.
Something
Moved in me
Shifted inside.
Not a breath apart
One sound
One beat
My feet
Rooted
Like theirs.
We rode
Into—the—Night.

LYING ON THE GROUND

clouds flowing across the moon
　　in rivers of air

my breath sleeps
　　feels its shape
　　and pulse

the wings of my back
　　relax

the light flickers
　　from day to night
　　and back again
　　setting up its own font
　　resetting my eyes

my fingers want to touch
　　my mouth to taste
　　what is so far away...

I feel the moisture
　　in my bones
　　the smile

MAGIC IS WHERE YOU FIND IT

Poetry out loud
Brings me into rhythms
And soundings deep.

I step into the bath
And fold myself
Almost in half.

Behind closed eyes
I see
Stars
And a redwood...

My lover comes in
For me.
Kisses my eyelids
Leaves.

After imponderable silence
I stand up
Bend
And a poem
Of gold
Flies
Out of
My middle.

A GIFT

Got up to go to the bathroom
In the middle of the night
Returning
Turned
On the light
To find my bed.
There on the pillow
With wings opened wide
    A labyrinth of orange and black
    A jigsaw of orange and white
A moth.
We slept side by side.

WINGS

In the bathroom
There are many big, legged things
Window open
I walk in
Many tiny ones too
Flown in
From the outdoor blue
A Room of Wings.

RECOGNITIONS

I saw a hummingbird today
Standing straight up in space
   Feathers fluttering so fast
   To look me in the face.

A shimmering surfeit of wings
   Like the hindu gods of arms and legs
   And kings
Created a thickening in the air
   Which caused my breastbone to tingle
   In recognition.

She was not bright green and red
   But a dull brown
   With orange sheen
   Plain, but
   Striking
   As a robin's egg
     In a nest.

She saw me
Spun around
Dove
Down
Straight
Behind a chair.

I could not see her anymore
But my body knew
She was there.

I am not alone
On the web of beings.

CLOTHES ARE UNDERRATED:
Or, This Dress Is Not Waterproof

Wedding dress trailing down the stairs
In falling folds
Across the hallway
Like shining water
Past the bathroom
And out the front door
Where more stairs greet it
But it is undaunted
And the shining sun
Helps it along.
The cloth ripples
Cloaks the stones
Refurbishes the little wounds
Tempts the man about
But not too soon.
Running right along with it
Of course is the veil
Of a net so fine
You can see right
Through it
So fine if you
Look into it
You see stars
And they both go hand in hand
Into the woods
So deep where darkness
Grows mushrooms of hope
And the moss of understanding
And out of those trees
Comes the ultimate goal—
A stream.

FOR ARWEN

I picked off a grey hair
from my blouse—
you must understand I
don't have many grey hairs.
It was curved and cut short
the day after my daughter gave birth.
I dropped it off my finger
and watched it float
and yield to the air
on its journey down.
I was there.
She danced and sang
the baby out.

FOR MY GRANDSON HUCK

I could have touched a fawn today
It seemed like that
Driving down my road
Off to the left, spots
Spots?
Spots in air
A deer
A little deer
A little little deer
A fawn
A young fawn
Littler still
Meconium
Clinging to his hind end
One, two days old
One, two hours?

I stopped and stared
He looked at me
As still as an
Old old tree
Not a breath
Eyes big, round
Not a blink
He did not move on tiny tiny legs
Too small to hold him
Seemed bones could break and then
There was that
Soft wispy fur soft
Golden golden
In the sun
Not a hair
Moving
In the breeze.
Not a hair
Moving
Not a hair...

I wanted to reach
I wanted to touch.

HOPE
For Emily Dickinson

Black crow
hovers o'er me
its shadow
covers me.

Tonight I look it
in the eye
I confess:
I am afraid of death.
"I release you!"
I cry.

It circles 'round
comes back
on me.

I roll over
feel my nipples press
the mattress.
My head slides
down the slope
of pillow.

Hot flash
like lightning—
a tiny moisture
on my temple.

Breathing.

I hear the rush of
feathers
leaving.

PLEASURES OF THE FLESH

Pleasures of the flesh
As it gets a little older
Not as tight
But soft and supple
Toweling myself up
And down
Under the arms
Down my breasts
Across the thigh
Cloth against skin
Skin moving from bone
Drops of water fall to the ground.

OCEANS

I'm swimming in something bigger than I am
Bigger than I ever thought to be
Floating on the ocean of the world.
Water swishing through my toes
Delicious me.
Swimming by a red barnacle
    a purple hair, a scarlet knee,
    chartreuse pick-up sticks
    a bobbing cork.
Trusting the jetsam floating by:
    the embryonic tide.
I did not know I had so much water inside.
The tide in my tears, my toes, my tits, my teeth—
The little soft spot where I don't know where I am.

Feel the water in your flesh
The water in your breath.

                The support of the water
                The support of the water
                The support of the water.

CRY JOY

Rushing down
Slushing down
Between my toes
Head let go
Feel the water
Cradling me
Silken on my skin
Speaks to water
I've forgotten
Inside.

And I
Replenished
And replete
Lie back
Feel my back
Release in
The water of all things:
　Into the lake
　Into the air above
　Into the mud below
　Into me in between.

I cry water for joy.

MY FARMERS' MARKET: 2009

I loved the market today—
The way the little girl
    crawled around
    on her belly
    in the fountain
while I ate tortillas with
    hard boiled duck eggs
    atop
    shredded lamb
    atop
    mole sauce.
And the newborn
sitting next to me
on her daddy's chest
was a wrap in a
blanket
    to ward
    off a chill.
Then there's the couple sitting
by my side from the big city
talking
about how their
eating here was
so ecological
so sustainable
so retainable—
Replaced later by
a walking couple
who remarked on, "Why
the flags?"
And I said,

27

"It's June.
It must be Flag Day.
And isn't it nice
I'm starting to
like the flag again."
And they grinned
and said,
"We're starting to
like our country again."

And the way the
deformed peaches
tasted.
And the African queen
selling her Shea Butter
amidst
dreadlocks and drums.
The ten-year-old kid
amidst the bongos
amidst his father
        playing guitar
and his father's father
        singing
with the little boy
        banging
        chewing his gum—
        not missing
        a lick of beat
        while his eyes drift
        off to the side
to a young teen girl
        doing cartwheels
        twirling hoops
        around her middle.
And the kohl-eyed woman
from the Middle East
with beads of amber
moonstone, turquoise, and jet.

My community 'tis of thee
"Sweet land of liberty."
Pastries, salmon
strawberry ices
baskets, flowers
and tie-dyed
saris—all for
reasonable
prices out
in the open air.
Folks ambling
to and fro
with colors sublime
mauve, puce
saffron, lime.
Aromas
calling your nose
from savory to sweet
pungent, piquant, spicy, and
slow.
"...and the living
is easy."

ALL WEEK

All week the night sky
Has hinted at red lavender.
The moon has shone out
All the stars
Except a few
Casting shafts of light
On the meadow.
Gone are the flesh
Of Cygnus and
Cassiopeia.
The crickets' hum
Caress the air
And I wonder what
Is to come
In the spaces
I have not foreseen.
I am enveloped
In a dark wool
Blanket.

THE MIRACLE OF WATER

I lifted up a glass
   In the middle of
   The night
It shocked me.
Water liquid water
Poured into my mouth.
I could feel its shape.
It became mine.
I could feel its taste.
Its clarity stained my tongue.
Its flowing slowly
   Filled me up—
   Water
   Is not a solid.
   It does not have
   Ordinary boundaries.
I can make it gurgle
        slosh
        spill
        spurt
        dribble
        drip
        EXPLODE.

It yields to me every time.
It has my full attention.
It soothes, refreshes, renews, cools
   gives solace
   comforts, pleasures, life.

All from one little drink
   In the middle of
   The night.
   When unguarded
   I tasted delight.

LATE NIGHT

The night sky
Is constantly
Wheeling
Away
From
Us

Gone are Orion
And the Pleiades

Now all that
Is left
Are a few scrabbly
scratches

A comma
A period, and a
Passing plane

VENUS
For Deidre

Venus rising on the horizon
Above the old oak tree
Apricot above
The foot of the earth
A backdrop for
The tracery of trees.

I go back to bed
Feeling soft flesh
Sink against linen sheets
I lie down instead of rise.

MUSINGS OF A MORNING

I. Tail Bone

I'm sitting on the edge of my chair
Slumped forward
Just up from sleep.
(You know the time
When the unconscious
Still rules
And writers write
Their morning papers.)
Nothing florid for me.
I feel
Simply bone
Not two
Not those ischial tuberosities
The cradle-rockers of the body.
This one is at the base of my spine
The central bone
The beginning of the tail
Bone.
Something mortal about bone.
Nothing like it.

II. Moth

My husband
Rescued a moth
From inside
Took it out
It flew up.
A bird
Dived.
Gone
In an instant
The image survived.

UNDERCOVER

Black snake with white bands
Spade-shaped head
Seamlessly moving from itself
Glistening forward.
Up the trough
By the rough-hewn fence
In and out
Of the nasturtiums.

A mother quail
With bobbing plume,
And eight babies bobbing
Fluffs on sticks,
Sees me
Dodges me
Runs
Around the bend
And under the flowered vines
Hanging
Over that ditch.

I KNOW NOW THAT...

Black petals
Taste bitter
   On the lips.
Long fingers
Smudge my cheeks
While ashes
Keep to their
   Own circle.
Darkness
Brings the
Gentlest things
And fear is
A thread through life.

OPENING THE LATCH

The squash rolls away
Off the ledge
   Below the window
As it was waiting
For the sun
To change
Its streaks of green
To yellow.

BITTERSWEET

The apples have fallen
Scented knives
Cross my nostrils

It is a hot hot day
As I struggle
    Reassuring myself
    Up on my bike
    Up an oscillating hill

Pale yellow
    Spills in shafts
    On my skin
The light has fallen.

THANKSGIVING

I have so much life around my house
Coyotes howl
Owls in their pas de deux calling
Fox, red and grey, weasels, raccoons
Bushy-tailed squirrels, chipmunks, and quail
Slithering snakes—garter, gopher, and king
Blind moles, burrowing badgers
Turkeys gobbling, deer prancing, skunky stinks
Feral cats, bobcats, roof rats, bats
Cougars in the valley, a peacock on the roof
Waddling possums 'cross my path
Horses of course
And multiple wings—
Blue birds, black birds, red-wings
Hummingbirds thrumming
Sparrows fighting, swallows swooping
Cedar waxwings, thrush, orioles
Cowbirds, grackles, chickadees, crows
Red-tailed and red-shouldered hawks
The great blue heron
Dark-shadowed vultures
Seeking their prey
Crawling creatures with bellies so low
Lizards leaping, frogs a-hopping, crickets whirring
Daddy longlegs dancing up the door
I have so much in life to be grateful for.

BREAKFAST NOOK

Sitting here with my four pumpkins
Watching the fog o'ertake the ridge
Dark shadows of trees
The clock ticks
The faucet drips
I feel silence
Creeping into
All the empty places

HOLIDAY (ENFORCED)

I have a cold
Time for sips of hot cups
(I never could say that right)
Not good at resting
Not good at sleeping
Did I tell you I don't like colds?
I'm not very good at it
I don't like yellow snot
So undignified
I don't like coughing
Rumping up my insides
I know this happens to everyone
I don't like the temperature swings
But why me?
Will I die?

I am noticing things differently
A lizard running on top of our stove
Tiny toes
A long-winged creature on the side of
A window
And no Tim this is not a
Termite. A little black snake
Slithering in the crack of
A stair
Washing my hands relentlessly
So my Sweetie doesn't get this,
Makes me feel like a disparate piece
Of germ, waiting to hop out
At someone.
Are you bored yet?

It's the waiting
It's the waiting to be well
The dislocation of the spirit.
I want to sit and write
that project
I'm excited about,
But my body says "no"
So I waffle and fart
And feel salt in my throat—
So many rinsings—
I am not the ocean.
The indignities
Of being human.

A brown and orange moth
Slowly flapping its wings
In the wind
Wobbles sideways
I haven't noticed such stuff
For awhile...

I notice a dead
Branch outside my
Studio window
It's been there since
July.
Breathing in
Through my
Right nostril
Sounds like
A giant storm.
All of the pictures on
The wall
Are tilted.

GOLD AT THE END OF THE POEM

Tonight
From lack of sleep
I took down the mistletoe
That had been hanging
Above our front door forgotten
For seven years.

As I pulled out the stick
Pin from its dark beam
I wondered if it too
Would fall down
From the change of
Something so embedded
In our daily life,
Would the house split
In half?
Would there still be kisses?
I shook a bit
But it was
Time...

Instead I looked at the
Almost white leaves
Bleached not from
The sun
Up in its dark place
But time
Time time time time
Time time time
And a thin red ribbon
The kind scissors
Are supposed to curl.
Untying it
A tiny
Gold bell
Fell.
It had been silent
All those years.

47

OUR COLLABORATION

CHRISTINA:

"Something different. A more interactive exchange between words and images." Deidre did a version, another, then another... Her images opened up a new dialogue with my craft. I began clarifying and cutting down certain poems. We had ardent conversations about design: intense, tricky critiquing sessions. Four years later, at the final push, we stepped back from each other, and each surrendered to our innate sense of what the book wanted.

Deidre sent me photos of her stitched panels, my verses laid in the settings she had created. I saw it: the images echoed the physical and emotional territory of my words. She had entered the dream-life of the poems, taking the magic and lighting it up with color. She had entered the shifting sea in all of us.

DEIDRE:

Christina's poems existed first, teasing my images into being. While continually reading and feeling her words, I began a journey that asked my work to follow her work. This path took me out of my comfort zone of the figurative into abstraction, where lay the very nature of the world. Night after night, day after day, season flowing into season, I sang her poems and found their colors, their contours and rhythms. This immersion in Christina's elements demanded a call-and-response between her spoken/written language and my visual language.

50

ACKNOWLEDGEMENTS

Christina and Deidre wish to thank the following colleagues, family, and friends who helped in the creation of this book:

Gwynn O'Gara and Arwen O'Reilly Griffith for editing and faith;

Isaiah Saxon, Katie Wilson, Nancy Burgess, and James Brisson for design consultation;

Monique Comacchio at Studio Ephemera for design consulting and typography;

Judith Bellamy for copyediting; Maria Hirano for proofreading;

Meara O'Reilly, Gina Blaber, and Rosemary Feitis for reading multiple drafts, and telling hard truths;

Saul Griffith for telling us to stick with what we know;

Hildegard Bachert, Linda Rubinstein, Corina Willette, Brian Selznick, and Laurie Whitehill Chong for artist's inspiration and support;

Steve Levine for making deadlines;

Salima Zimmerman, Nancy Carroll, Patti Trimble, Kathleen Langermann, Bob Poole, Marg Starbuck, Bill Boykin, Nancy Atlas, Nan Whitney, Andrea Dunlap, Sam Barry, Jackie Abrams, Patricia Burleson, Kris McDermet, Susan Osgood, and Lauri Richardson for heartfelt encouragement;

Arwen O'Reilly Griffith, Deborah Kruger, and Al Karevy for photography;

Peter Koch for inspiring us to change design elements;

Mark Swingle's guidance at GSL;

... and Christina's bathtub.

CHRISTINA ISOBEL is a poet, playwright, producer, and performer. Her passion for experiential, immersive poetry began in 1985 when she created a poetry/dance concert, *Ecstatic Indian Poetry and Dance*, featuring Robert Bly and Indian classical dancer, Neena Gulati, intertwining words and dance with tabla and sitar. First presented at Harvard and MIT, the concert traveled to California, Maine, and Maryland. Isobel went on to co-found the Loading Zone Theater in Santa Rosa, California. Later she wrote, produced, directed, and choreographed the lyric play, *Skeleton Woman: A Dance with the Dark*, inspired by an Inuit fairytale. She now performs her own poems, weaving sound and gesture with the words.

Isobel lives in San Francisco and Sonoma County.

Pioneering in the medium of thread on layered fabric, DEIDRE SCHERER has exhibited her work since 1979, including solos at the Baltimore Museum of Art; the Brattleboro Museum & Art Center in Vermont; the Hebrew Union College-Jewish Institute of Religion Museum in New York City; and the Maltwood Art Museum in Victoria, British Columbia. She was featured in the film, *Holding Our Own*, which screened at the Museum of Fine Arts, Boston. Her work is on the cover of the best-selling book, *When I Am an Old Woman I Shall Wear Purple*, and the poetry anthology, *Threads of Experience*. She wrote about her art's evolution in *Deidre Scherer: Work in Fabric and Thread*.

Scherer received the American Academy of Hospice and Palliative Medicine's 2008 *Humanities Award* and the Rhode Island School of Design's 2010 *Alumni Association Award for Artistic Achievement*, as well as fellowships from the Vermont Arts Council and the Open Society Institute.

CODA: OUR BREATH

I walk in the silence of the trees
A journey of the breath
Into the heart
Out to release.
Moss growing up my ankles
One step, two
Straight as trunks
Branching
From my spine
My legs move
Bark a'cracklin'.
Out the air goes
Through my mouth
Curves in space
Follows currents
Between two worlds
Mending the particular
By connecting to the whole.
Leaves a canopy
'Round my shoulders
Sticking out my ears.
Now I know trees
Are the lungs
Of this world.

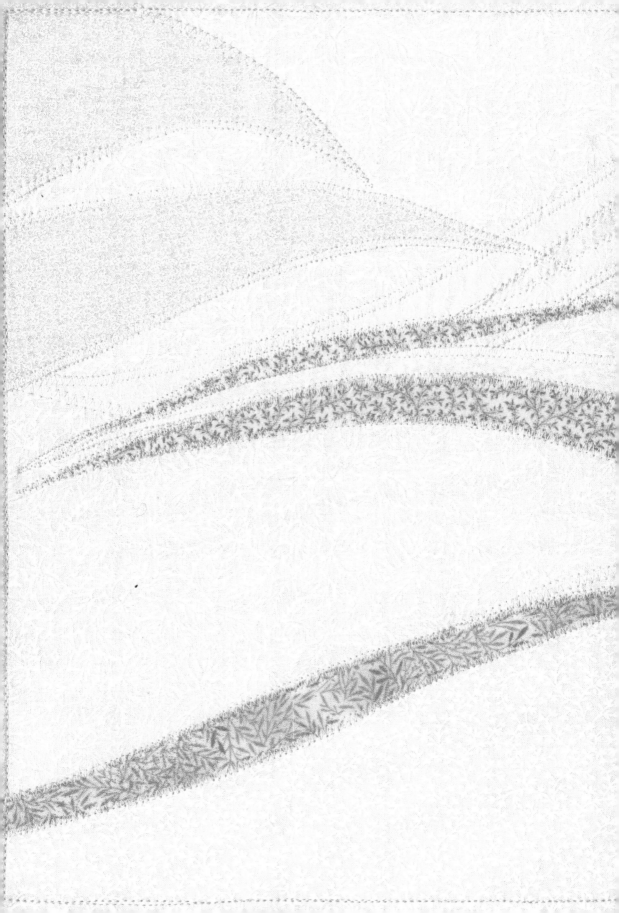